conditions apply

Copyright © 2020 Mary Rykov

Except for the use of short passages for review purposes, no part of this book may be reproduced, in part or in whole, or transmitted in any form or by any means, electronically or mechanically, including photocopying, recording, or any information or storage retrieval system, without prior permission in writing from the publisher.

The publisher gratefully acknowledges the support of the Canada Council for the Arts and the Ontario Arts Council. The publisher is also grateful for the financial assistance received from the Government of Canada.

Cover design: Val Fullard

Library and Archives Canada Cataloguing in Publication

Title: some conditions apply : poems / Mary Rykov.
Names: Rykov, Mary, 1953– author.
Series: Inanna poetry & fiction series.
Description: Series statement: Inanna poetry & fiction series
Identifiers: Canadiana (print) 20200204424 | Canadiana (ebook) 20200204432 |
ISBN 9781771337656   (softcover) | ISBN 9781771337663 (epub) |
ISBN 9781771337670 (Kindle) | ISBN 9781771337687 (PDF)
CLASSIFICATION: LCC PS8635.Y56 S66 2020 | DDC C811/.6—dc23

Printed and bound in Canada

Inanna Publications and Education Inc.
210 Founders College, York University
4700 Keele Street, Toronto, Ontario M3J 1P3 Canada
Telephone: (416) 736–5356   Fax (416) 736–5765
Email: inanna.publications@inanna.ca Website: www.inanna.ca

some conditions apply

poems

Mary Rykov

inanna poetry & fiction series

INANNA Publications and Education Inc.
Toronto, Canada

Contents

1.

befor[e]wards & afters	3
post-shooting sonnet	4
summer doesn't notice	5
jíbaro	6
puertorriqueña	7
Christiansted, USVI, May 2019	10
bless with promise each sunrise	11
take me home	12
trading places	13
routine surgery	14
The last time you phone me	15
cottonwood	16
Cadaver Number 929-75	18
suite in the shadow of death's valley	21
Choice	23

2.

sonata	27
n = 24	28
music forces its way out	31
Re: "*An Die Musik*/To Music"	32
homage to music therapy	33
Failing suicide	34
Case Closed	36

music while dying	37
music in time	38
this song	39
I am	40
singing Cohen	41
Tosca	42
music remembers	43

3.

Taraxacum officinale	47
falling	48
Apple Cake	49
Bubba	51
Translation and Interpretation 101	52
masquerade	54
it all starts at the kitchen table	55
beyond one summer journey	57
happy hour moon over miami	58
stories	59
the Siren's tale	61
some conditions apply	62

4.

with resolve to resolve	65
s[p]in cycle	66

invigilation	67
diethylstilbestrol (DES)	68
questions before and after understanding	69
a postphilosophy rant	70
roads to refuge	71
silence	73
How to have a good death in Canada circa 2020	74
negotiating death	76
writing prompt	78
poem paths	79
the view from w/here	80
Notes	81
Gratitude	86

*If I am not for myself,
who will be for me?*

*If I am only for myself,
what am I?*

*If not now,
when?*

—Hillel (circa 110 BCE – 10 CE)

1.

befor[e]wards & afters

hunger
like thirsty fish

craving
like vitamin deficiency

collision
like keys in locks

opportunity
like flotsam

headlights
like deer in a jet stream gaze

gaze
like the never-neverland prince

lawn pucky
like that of his horse

never-neverland
like barely manageable wreckage

wreckage
like wind-tossed plastic

songs inside eggs
like portals to always

post-shooting sonnet

Sparrows hop
the sultry pool deck
scrounging snack crumbs
while squeals and screams
belly laughs and belly flops
flips and plops
punctuate
splashes

Crickets chirp
and birds beg
in flux, in fright,
and in the all
and in the nothing
that changes

summer doesn't notice

Cicadas complain overhead
Leaves crunch underfoot

Conkers break open
where they fall

Light dies early now
with chill of evening air

Summer blinks
and flees

jíbaro

Out my window
caña de azúcar
cut with machetes
cleared by tractors

I jump up and down
to wave you close
to see smiles
under straw hats

Outstretched arms
feed me sweets
while back home
your own babes need basics

When I call you jíbaro
means I call you LOVE

puertorriqueña

1.

Graduate school fieldwork
finds me at the Jacob Perlow Hospice
of the Beth Israel Medical Center
where the Lubavitcher Rebbe
Mendel Menachim Shneerson
lies dying on another hospital unit
not the hospice unit
because a moshiach doesn't die

Well-wishers crowd the entrance
Children sing in the park
The moshiach-mobile
circles the hospital block,
speakers blaring

Inside I know an easy rapport
with many New York City patients
because like Kotter's Epstein
I am a proud Puerto Rican Jew

I'm a Jewish spic!
My girlish pride
chastised by
Don't say that, you
can't say that, don't you
ever let me hear you
say that

Tasked to prepare a music therapy
self-portrait for class, I improvise
in binary rondo form a conversation
between my namesake María Elena song
and a classic Chassidic niggun

2.

So, what is a Puerto Rican Jew?

My mother would tell you
Puerto Rican Jews
live in summer heat
all four seasons
no lilacs, no apples

My father would tell you
Puerto Rican Jews
live in a paradise
far from Gestapo selections

Some Puerto Rican Catholics
will tell you they too are Jews
descended from Mallorcan *chuetas*
forcibly Christianized in 1391
who, in 1508, hitch
an Age-of-Discovery ride
with Ponce de León
only needing to hide again
from the Inquisition
in the New World

3.

I will tell you in luscious color
how Yiddish and Spanish merge
in the ear as lullaby
while the surf drones
and the *coquí* sings
through thick air
warm like a blanket

I will tell you the connection
for this *puertorriqueña* to Puerto Rico
is like the *sabra* to Israel
with irrational tribal ties
that won't let go

Christiansted, USVI, May 2019

Despite that state-side fixers fly in
after Irma and María,
rooftops still FEMA-blue-tarp broken
two years on

A redux oil refinery sports
new management, new name
same get-rich-quick
tricks

More state-side fly-in crews
exploit laid-back locals
for fun and profit while density swells
pre-existing social-safety-net cracks

Prices soar
and taxis fleece naive tourists
who learn how to haggle
before they leave

And them hard-workin' boys
beyond reproach
let off hard-playin' steam
unchecked

Plastic fast-food litter,
broken glass, butts and beer caps
now adorn sea life, beaches,
and road-side ditches

bless with promise each sunrise

In photos Mother thinks
I'm old enough to witness
                        heaps of limb discards blur
                  with naked skeletons bunked wild-eyed

Beyond hide-and-seek I play out
Papa's holos kaustos
                        burning whole his legacy
                          as Anne Frank hiding

Hiding and acting out in turns
how cats pounce cowering mice
                              adrenaline fuels
                              ear-plumed sleep

Africans rough
unholy horror
                        sink in the Middle Passage
                            cry out through time

withFirstNationsSalem*MedzYeghern*BiafraRwanda
DarfurIrelandPalestineAfghanistanSyriaYemen…
                            Molten grief in the heart
                                of dormant Pompeis
    under whose shadow
    sorrow inflates with duty—
                            duty to play again, rejoice
                    and bless with promise each sunrise

take me home

Sunlit sparkles
float like feathers
hide cruel beauty

Cry when they try
to clothe me in
itchy-scratchy warm wool

Cry when they try
to send me outside
to play in cold slush

Frost-bitten hands and feet
tongue frozen to pipes
they say not to lick

¡Mamá, tengo frío, tengo frío!
She says she knows, but
she won't take me home

trading places

the new house   at home
another beingness   in space

purging   painting
fresh coats on   old dreams bleeding

into new reverie   leaving
losing   letting go

opening   embracing
the new   muscles strain

under boxes   boxes   boxes
boxes   and more   boxes

unpacking   searching
the butterfly   for the pupa's soul

routine surgery

Saw it off here, hammer it in there,
sew you back up
and you're good to go
with a new post-surgical leg
that doesn't work

Blood loss and stretched nerves,
this surgical luck of the draw
no one anticipates, but
surely you expect to feel better,
better and stronger by now

Eight weeks out, pain
so bad in burning hues
of purplish black that gnaws,
twists and pulls so hard
leaves you numb and breathless,
blurring sickness of pain
with sickness of pain meds

All a poor body can do
is make friends
with the patient compassion
only pain can teach

the last time you phone me

You catch me alone cleaning
the bagless vacuum filter   We talk
as I dislodge packed-in detritus
with a bristle brush   Much time

has passed since we last spoke
and even more since I cleared this filter
Stubborn particles protest as I disturb
dust from complacency   You say

your prognosis changed
from years to months,
your estimated date of death
nearer than you hoped for or feared

You say *it is what it is*
as dirt flies furiously
in all directions, stinging
my eyes and throat

cottonwood

As billowy tufts fall
you ask about death,
you want to prepare

I comfort you with
a gentle lie-of-omission,
white as cottonwood,

that dying is serene
like this downy wool,
but

in your chaotic passing
only death can bless
the end of agony

And in each spring blizzard
of cottonwood drift
I remember all this

with sorrow
filling the void
now sweetened

by your daughter
who mothers her daughter
named, of course, for you

And all this I remember
in each spring blizzard
of cottonwood drift

Cadaver Number 929-75

Tension simmers
this music I speak

Pregnant with the world,
babies pop from me
& as I spin their cradles
from my own gut-string
my mind splits open
like a robin's egg cracked
but still singing

Enslaved by feathers and blood
on my windowsill, holy water wells
like stigmata in my palms   Lonely as god
before the invention of colour, I leave
only land behind after metaphors fail

The mountain presence rejects nothing
I bumslide down these mountains
& splat into the sea
already so full with bones and miracles,
my closed-quartz throat
a bloodstone-dark jewel of history

Swirling in the cold prick of bubbles
on my underbelly, I sink
reach centre & roil
in its wake

Only my lover sees me
with human ? eyes, eyes that stain
the sky bloody with Betelgeuse
I approach this lover so rough with need
that by day's end his empty scrotum sags,
but first we fall thrashing
like fish in saltchuck

The firemen will say
they must have smoked in bed
just for godsake don't step there
where slugs ooze viscid mess

When my film splinters white
I do not wake because
I am already married
to a different dangerous man
who rattles the stones
in my skull's cavity
& scrapes my knees
on ice-cleaved ground

A husband whose hammer head
indents my occipital bone
as he shatters me
& splatters my blood

No care can efface this Janus-pain love
that barks while the sun stands still
in its empty ring of frozen trumpets
& love, love turns to milk stone

Pulled lifeless from Furry Creek,
they identify Cadaver Number 929-75
and Mrs Pat Lowther
as one and the same

How dare they doubt me,
doubt I could be this husk

suite in the shadow of death's valley

1.

She looks up from behind
the loaded fork en route to her mouth

Sometimes it takes every ounce of self-control
to keep from murdering him in his sleep

2.

Eventually he dies
of natural causes

demanding   everything
commanding everyone

struggling to control
his last breath

3.

Six weeks later she sees him
in the closet with the light on

wearing one of those Japanese kimonos
he likes so much

It's so upsetting   she sobs
I want him out of here

4.

We are a small family
their daughter explains

but what we lack in size
we make up for in dysfunction

Dysfunction she describes
as the curse of an evil eye

beyond bad genes and denial
that follows ancestors

from the Old World to the New
without stopping to clear customs

Choice

When it's over, I don't want to wonder
if I have made of my life something particular, and real.
I don't want to find myself sighing and frightened,
or full of argument.
—Mary Oliver, "When Death Comes'"

Sometimes a life grows
into its death;
sometimes death
takes a life
and tears
it asunder.
On any given rain-soaked morning
the choice remains
how to brighten the thunder.
When it's over, I don't want to wonder

why I don't nurture
acceptance
for loss
of person, roles, station,
health and function—
those cards of the deal.
Most important
to know and feel
if I have made of my life
something particular, and real.

Patience welcomes
all floods as trust
rescues hope
like sunlit
singing
with all senses heightened
healing the dank, dark muck
such that even when
I can no longer do as I might and
don't want to find myself sighing and frightened.

Passing the world like an orange
to a child on the journey
from dust to dust
to ponder how it ends
—for stop it must—
with innocent grace
let me face this choice,
this choice to be songful
and targeted
or full of argument.

2.

sonata

Tones in simultaneous fluid
promise repose in suspended space

then detour to a deceptive cadence
With myths we yearn to story the course

that fords the bridge of transformed time
in new designs of familiar comfort

like cozy sweaters by magic unwound
on a different day and distant shore

n = 24

or maybe 23 or 25 or 26
difference between accuracy and truth
incites complexity

Magic spells
or maybe counts
the same way we do

Like the speeding cyclist
who stops traffic to kiss
the startled jaywalker

we create islands to ride
while the ride is good until
harsh words sever meat from bone

We function
in historical moments
hysterical mindsets

Without humour
we die
of despair

Without despair
we die
in peace

Without music
we die
of meaninglessness

Without art to tell us
how meaningless we may be
we lose all reason

Reality through tailspin lens
of pure song and metaphor
mirrors objects closer than they appear

This journey
longing for unattainable fulfillment
never knows its route or destination

We forget memory is disruptive—
how easier we imagine
than remember

We stand
as the judge
enters the courtroom

We clap
as the conductor
ascends to the podium

We gasp
as the baby falls
from his mother's arms

to death   Nothing
more can be said
yet

everything is expressible
all is translatable
in silence

In our duty to tell tales, complicit
with witness and remembrance
of experience beyond words,

good and bad endings
include the backstory
underbelly of the whale

Grief aching poignant want
spends generous gratitude
for all that crosses its path

Truth sprouts
like small-crevice wildflowers
after a rain

in 24 perfect petals
or maybe 23
or 25 or 26

music forces its way out

Familiar strangeness ripples
perpetual change in fluid motion

audible landscape
the flip side of air

breath of statues
inaudible

silence in paintings
unspeakable

Reveals the unknowable
where all language ends

Such holy sounds of intangible touch
unbinds and embodies

Indeterminate, primal
music forces its way out

Re: "*An Die Musik*/To Music"

Dear Mr Rilke,

This spontaneous response to your
lived experience of music written
in Frau Hanna Wolff's 1918 guestbook
after the concert you hear
in her Munich parlour

is neither studied
nor composed   Perhaps
you consider such work
                      unworthy

which may explain why
you choose not to publish
this unintended poem
of humble birth?

homage to music therapy

Rocking and crying
your soul in tatters, pain flows
through a shattered mind
We sing and bring you solace
making music of your moans

Failing suicide

Sixteen months ago I swallow
every pill in the medicine cabinet—
my twelve-year-old solution
The docs re-start my arrested heart,
but they say my brain
will never recover

So I lie in a hospital bed
eight more months
"awaiting placement,"
contractures splinted
and drugged, drugged, drugged
because I seizured once
and could be so agitated at times

Next I transfer
to long-term "total care"
where I say *Enough*—
tear the splints off
with my one functional hand
and fling them across the room

Again I say *Enough*—
pull the feeding tube
out of my stomach
and all the king's horses

and all the king's men
can't get that tube
back inside me again because
Enough, I say, *Enough*

I hold up my head,
smile and laugh,
eat on my own,
say what sounds like *hi*
and mouth *'bye*

All the while
I beat our drum and sing,
then start to walk
and talk and say
what happened

Case Closed

The old woman slouches
chin to chest, waiting
as others fill the room

The eager new therapist
mirrors her softness—
Hello Mrs Vernicke, good to meet you

Mrs Vernicke raises her head
meets the young woman's eyes—
I'm going to die soon is all she says

The startled novice kisses her cheek
That's okay—
is all she answers

Mrs Vernicke stops eating,
never speaks again,
dies within weeks

The therapist writes a discharge summary,
mails it with condolences to the family,
then moves the Vernicke chart

to the "inactive" file
in the bottom drawer
of the tall, green cabinet

music while dying

Listen in awe,
witness

Witness beauty
flicker

in the perfect stillness
of a blissful sleeping smile

> Hearing the progression
> cycle through
> I   iii   IV   I
> I   vi   ii V^7
> may be correct but unhelpful
> when tremors, blinks, moans
> and sighs dictate
> music options
>
> Technical skill alone
> fails elegant grace—
> sacred connections
> and profound intentions
> redolent with holy bonds

Listen   witness
A simple song cradles

Buffers the suffering
of ultimate severing

music in time

Reverie floats in gossamer
as sound lingers, juxtaposed
with exterior clocks

Bands together
through dance and drill

Metric pulse as music glue
renders wrong tones
plausible

when sounding together
at the right time

this song

I take the threads
of a young spider's web
and make you a cloak
to hold you from cold
I weave it well
cast a magic spell
to keep you warm
and shield you from harm

l grow you a garden
of rainbow-faced pansies
who laugh and dance
and sing in the sun
and sway with the wind
and smile while you watch
They grace
our table with love

I go
down to the meadow
and fill your pillow
with soft willow leaves
I rest my head
upon your chest
and sing you this song
as we fall into sleep

I am

Want me, I'm a precious gem
Chase me, I am the wind
Smell me, I'm the wildwood flower
Follow me, I am the sun

Need me, I'm hope
Trust me, I am the light
Take me, I'm yours
Love me, I am the night

    Carry me, I'm tired
    Hold me, I'm a frightened child
    Steady me, I'm weak
    Pardon me, I've been blind

    Fill me, I'm empty
    Mend me, I've been torn
    Plant me, watch me grow
    like an untold babe awaiting to be born

singing Cohen

We sang your honey
when our youth
was new   We lean

this way
forever,
travel blind

Tosca

We were hoping
you might think
things through,
try to get over it

No matter your
beloved Cavaradossi
lies executed
at your feet,

Liberty is in the air,
Art will prevail
and you, luscious diva,
can love again

Floria, stop! Let
fly your faith to unfetter hope
Just this time, please,
please—don't jump

music remembers

As birthright,
joy, frustration, solace, refuge, nemesis,
light and darkness, complacency and compulsion,

music measures movement through time
as yardstick for growth and change
played out in moments remembered

Music as teacher
of hearing, listening, thinking,
feeling, doing, meaning, healing

Musical being—
creaturely, mutable,
necessary as breathing

3.

Taraxacum officinale

Golden globes
sporting on her

windowsill
in the chill

of winter
improvise

in the key
of February

falling

I am falling, I think,
in love with you, but
on reflection reason
I'm just falling
for morning birdsong
and wild spring flowers
in the wadi beyond your gate

Apple Cake

I slice six tart Northern Spy apples
into an oiled 8x8-inch bake pan
then sprinkle sugar
dark with cinnamon

    Yes, Ma
    I wash the apples well
    but I don't peel away
    vitamins and fibre
    in long unbroken spirals
    nor do I iron cotton bed sheets
    while watching old television movies
    on Sunday afternoons

I beat
one cup of sugar
into three eggs
with a half cup of oil
and a teaspoon of pure vanilla extract
using an old rotary hand beater
just like yours

    Yes, Ma
    I preheat the oven
    to 350°F
    but these days
    we call it 175°C

Into this liquid I sift
a cup of flour
with two teaspoons of baking soda
using a tin wheel sifter
with a red knob on the handle
just like yours   Then I mix
this fluid batter using
an old wooden spoon
with nicks and stains
just like yours

    Yes, Ma
    I run the rolling pin over
    a paper bag filled with
    one cup of shelled walnuts
    just like you did

I fold
these walnut pieces
into the batter
and pour everything over
the crisp tart apples waiting
in the pan now ready
for the oven

    Yes, Ma
    after one hour
    sublime harmonies
    of vanilla and cinnamon
    blend to perfection
    just like you

Bubba

rocks back
and forth,
to and fro,

slaps at pain
slicing
her knees

We try to hold her gnarled hands
that once soothed
our fevered childhood brows,

the same hands that brewed
chicken soup with noodles
made from scratch

She pulls away and shakes
her scolding finger: *don't*
get old, don't get old

don't get old
don't get
old

Translation and Interpretation 101

Variations in **substance** **are not very important.**

All cases of interpretation **and even parody—insofar as** **highly perspicuous** **suffice**s to **identify** **tics of a certain** **fact** **with** **more** **metaphor.**

To understand this point better, see in Lepschy 2981 (456-7) the sentence 'His friend could not see the window.' Lepschy observes that this sentence allows for twenty-four different Italian translations, which may combine in a different way a series of choices, namely (i) whether **the friend** is male or female, (ii) whether *could not* should be understood as an imperfect or a past definite tense, (iii) whether window should be understood as the window **of a** room (*finestra*) or of a train (*finestrino*) or of a counter, as in a **bank teller's window** (*sportello*). Lepschy **is the first to admit that** the twenty-four solutions are only potential, because within the **context** only one **would be appropriate.** But this **leaves us with** three **problems,** which are very different from one another to contain all the possible...

masquerade

You disguise yourself as a bag of trash
stepping through two leg holes
cut into a green plastic garbage bag
stuffed with crumpled newspaper,
a pipe cleaner twist-tied at your neck

I decorate you
with gutted muffin cups,
fat crumbs, grape stems,
candy bar wrappers
and for good measure
a rusting banana peel

I disguise myself
as the good-witch-of-the-woods
and because of the mask and wand
no one knows who I really am
as I dance through the crowd
granting three wishes
to those brave enough
to confide in me

it all starts at the kitchen table

Amidst smashed potatoes
congealed gravy
shrivelled peas
dysfunctional reports
of the day parsed
into opinions, positions
and unfulfilled desires
of being naked in a poem

Arguably who as subject
the object of whom
from which misplaced antecedents
no less subordinate
to the dangled phrase
mangle diction
for even the easiest
of participles rendered

senseless and uncaring
to any discerning palate
whilst Father conjugates
just for the I, you,
he, she, we and they,
the *it* of it all that sends
Mother running for succour
to the bottle she finds

empty, sucked dry
on a dare from the twins
brawling over who gets
the last of the cupcakes
and thus what starts
innocuously enough
is endlessly sentenced
to run on and on

beyond one summer journey

Across the bucket seat divide
sunlight filters
through windshield
bug splat

Engine noise over whines
thick with smells
of ice cream melt
and wet towels, they know

the only long-term guarantee
for loving each other
is to marry
somebody else

happy hour moon over miami

She sees on his smooth glans
old disappointments weep
with petty judgments,

tachycardia explained
as depression, anxiety
and bad food

Blaming him on and off
forty years
for not trying,

she croons
the tune
into submission

as stinging jellyfish
with consumptive last hurrahs
wash up on sand

slurping the oyster bare—
the one only love can shuck
and toss back to the sea

stories

Thanks for the stories whose plot twists
jump out
from behind potted palms
in hotel lobbies

Thanks for the stories whose subtexts
lie about their age and weight,
wear the wrong shade of lipstick
and pad their bras with old clichés

Thanks for the story protagonists
who text while driving
and don't believe
in turn signals

Thanks for the supporting characters
who ramble through frozen food aisles
choosing too much sodium, sugar, and transfats
while talking with their mouths full

Thanks for the genre stories
who leave rings around the bathtub
and never replace
empty toilet paper rolls

Thanks for the first-person narrators
who arrive too early,
stay too late
and tweet too much

Thanks for the second-person narrators
who drink indiscriminately
before noon—
you know who you are

Thanks for the third-person narrators
who are spooked by climate change
and can't be trusted
with nuclear codes

Thanks for all the stories
these stories tell

the Siren's tale

A thrashing fish struggling to spit free
of the hook meets a rudderless boat

adrift between winds and currents
vying to control its destiny

Along comes a gentle man who,
delighting in her food and drink,

fears the dangerous
comforts of her refuge

>He says   *I just wanna be friends*
>She says   *stop kissing my mouth*

some conditions apply

Stop calling her: Eurydice
doesn't give a duck's dick about you
now that she's crossed
the sweet sonic boom

Besides, you think nouns are just things
so you only fart verbs
cuz you figure that's where
all the action is

No, she doesn't racial profile
romantic prospects
but some conditions apply—
like not dating monotonously

Me? make my words
thick and rich
shaken, stirred
and crispy

4.

with resolve to resolve

When beginning, begin
Strive and stretch
Reach for growth
in vibrant new ways

Strive and stretch
when earth turns inward
In vibrant new ways
days shorten and shiver

When earth turns inward
return to yourself
Days shorten and shiver
in steadfast return

Return to yourself
Recover redemption
in steadfast return
as courageous reboot

Recover redemption
Reach for growth
as courageous reboot
When beginning, begin

s[p]in cycle

Task flowing water

to cleanse crumbs

as sponge bloated

with flaws and faults

we cast to the sacred see

seeking mercy

for erosion wreaked

on holy shores

We sin

We return

We repent

We repeat

invigilation

Count down the time—
white foraminafera on green
the colour of afternoon seas
through sun

Sneezes syncopate
windowless silence where
students erase and re-write
multiple choice guesses

Thank you miss
Have a nice summer
Take good care miss

Chalk dust
like snow drifts
to my knees

diethylstilbestrol (DES)

*from The American Heritage®
Dictionary of the English Language,
4th Edition:*

n. A synthetic nonsteroidal
substance, C18H20O2,
having estrogenic properties and
used ... to ... prevent miscarriage
but is no longer prescribed for
these cases because of the
occurrence of reproductive
abnormalities and cancers in the
offspring of women so treated

*from Wiktionary, Creative Commons
Attribution/Share-Alike License:*

n. An orally-active synthetic
nonsteroidal oestrogen, first
synthesized in 1938 and
withdrawn in the 1970s on being
identified as a teratogen

*wordnik.com/words/
diethylstilbestrol*

DES robs
them empty
in gestation

They make no babies
change no diapers
read no stories

check no homework
pack no lunches
happy no birthdays

no graduations
no weddings
no grandchildren

Childless parents
who nurture
vicariously

justify this loss
as their gift
bestowed

upon a festering
overcrowded
planet

questions before and after understanding

What remains unfinished
in dreams from which we wake

haunts space between absence and presence
at the crossroads of here and there

Truths we show and truths we hide
Memories we recall and those we neglect

Moments between then and now illumine
polarities we choose to balance

a postphilosophy rant

Blame it on capricious gods
Greeks and Sumerians fabricate
to explain the wiles of humankind
and impose order
on the common chaos of being

With vestiges today in
objective acceptance
the consequence of breaching
enlightened evidence is ostracism

Now as then
the embodied paradox
TRUTH = truths

No crying foul, no charges
of sophistry, relativism, rhetoric
can obscure this monism forever

So, let's just get on with it
and return the pantheons
to their rightful frolic

roads to refuge

1.

Thou-shalt-nots
moult cast-offs
like beads hanging on
but strung out and lost

to stinking seas
as jetsam tossed
and flotsam beached
on distant shores

2.

Sometimes the women
dance prayers to the stars
bathe in waterfalls
sing libations

bleed together under full moons
their quickenings a promise,
promise of destiny through a fire
that does not consume

Only the Miriams,
empty and barren,
never reach
promised lands

3.

Help us: we need,
we need comfort—
our safety stolen
by this past we carry

parched and blistered,
stopping only
to pile the cairns
for our dead

silence

Students better off illiterate
cry out for rescue, suffocate
under crumbling rubble—

shoddy concrete
around rebar steel supports
too few to matter

May 13th we hear voices
   May 14th they grow faint
      May 15th we hear silence

Pooh Bear Mickey Mouse backpacks piled high the price of expansion for lives never guaranteed to be safe

How to have a good death in Canada circa 2020

1. Don't be poor

2. Don't have poor parents, relatives or friends

3. Don't be homeless; better still, own property and cars

4. Increase your likelihood of receiving comprehensive end-of-life care in home or hospital by having an end-stage cancer diagnosis with a clear prognosis of three months or less

5. Increase your likelihood of accessing comprehensive end-of-life care treatment for your end-stage cancer by living in a large urban centre, not in rural or remote Canada

6. Don't have one or more of the following: heart or lung disease, dementia, neurological disorder and any other condition associated with a lingering or unclear prognosis

7. Don't have a debilitating, intractable mental illness

8. Die on time; failure to die in a timely manner may result in transfer from your end-of-life care unit or program

9. Choose to buy your one-way tourist death exit abroad at your discretion, or hire a lawyer to argue your assisted death case at home

10. To purchase your one-way tourist death exit abroad or to hire a lawyer, see Item 1, above

negotiating death

The curious jackdaw steals
shiny bits to build disorderly nests,
plays in the abyss, braves nightmares
to emerge enlightened

> Chiron healing his wounds?
> Hydra growing uncontrolled subtexts?
> Jacob wrestling the nameless angel?

> Maybe mutable Proteus, wary
> of mammon and false gods?

> Or Sisyphus happy, redeemed
> by his rock?

Our days as handbreadths
ripple through wind
while dead hostages fail
to emerge in real time,

victims forever captive
even as these words form
on the same page that joins
reader with writer in story wrested

from the dark
haggling the deal,
negotiating with the dead, with death
but never with our own death

Won't you sing to us
some pretty bits
to flutter
in this breeze?

writing prompt

Using freshly moulted feathers
from fledgling sparrows
write your name
as it appeared
in yesterday's
obituary

Let them squawk,
don't stop

Keep both hands moving
across the sky

poem paths

Down collective mindshafts
nuggets of grace
hewn from rock face

ancient humus-
words morph
crystalline

Brilliant beauty
beckons poemseed
shared bounty

we till, tend
& echo
through time

the view from w/here

Bashō wakes!
>returns from
>his journey
>through withered fields

>sings me
>to the edge
>of breath

Bashō says—
>*you can't take it with you*
>*so write it*
>*now*

Notes

"befor[e]wards & afters," a Tony Hoagland-Rumi mash-up.

"post-shooting sonnet" distills the aftermath of 23 July 2018 on Toronto's Danforth Avenue.

The Puerto Rican "*jíbaro*"—roughly translated as peasant farmer (and ruder referents)—descended from survivors who escaped the Spanish conquistadors by fleeing to the mountains. The *jíbaro* holds traditional farming knowledge and cultural resilience. The poem references the closing lines of "Puerto Rican Obituary" by Nuyorican poet, Pedro Pietri (1934-2004), "to be called negrito / Means to be called LOVE."

A "*puertorriqueña*" is a woman born on Puerto Rico, the colonized Caribbean island called Borinquén by its Indigenous Taíno inhabitants. The Lubavitch movement of Orthodox Jews believed their rabbi was the *moshiach* [Hebrew: messiah]. Spic is an offensive term for a Spanish-speaking person from Central America, South America, or the Caribbean. The popular love song, "María Elena," was written by Lorenzo Barcelata in 1932. A *niggun* [Yiddish: melody] is a wordless traditional melody of the Ashkenazi Jewish sect. *Chuetas* [Spanish: descendants of Mallorcan convert Jews], also known as *converso* or *marrano*, refers to individuals from the Sephardic Jewish sect who converted to Catholicism during the Spanish Inquisition while secretly continuing to practise their Jewish faith. DNA testing confirms Jewish ancestry for some Catholics in Puerto Rico and throughout the Caribbean. The Puerto Rican *coquí* is a tree frog that sounds like a songbird. A *sabra* is a native-born Israeli.

"The last time you phone me" in memoriam Faroqh Monajem.

"cottonwood" in memoriam Elsie (Denise) Hammond.

The "Cadaver Number 929-75" cento quotes words from Pat Lowther (1935-1975) as well as others who wrote about her life and about her death by spousal homicide:

Brooks, Toby. *Pat Lowther's Continent: Her Life and Work.* Charlottetown: gynergy books, 2000.

Greco, Heidi and Ellen S. Jaffe, editors, with texts by Christine Lowther, Toby Brooks and Carolyn Zonailo. *A Tribute to Pat Lowther on What Would Have Been Her 75th Birthday.* Toronto: Living Archives of the Feminist Caucus of the League of Canadian Poets, 2011.

Lowther, Pat. *This Difficult Flowring.* Illustrations by S. Slutsky. Vancouver: Very Stone House, 1968.

Lowther, Pat. *Milk Stone.* Ottawa: Borealis Press, 1974.

Lowther, Pat. *The Collected Works of Pat Lowther.* Edited by Christine Wiesenthal. Edmonton: NeWest Press, 2010.

"Choice," a glosa poem from "When Death Comes" by Mary Oliver (1935–2019) in *New and Selected Poems, Volume One* (Boston: Beacon Press, 2004); and after Edgar Lee Masters, "Tomorrow is My Birthday" in *Spoon River Anthology* (Urbana, IL: University of Illinois Press, 1992).

The deceptive cadence in "sonata" refers to the end of a phrase in Western tonal music when closure is interrupted and does not resolve as is typically expected.

The "n" of "n = 24" refers to the sample subset of a population in research statistics.

"music forces its way out" loosely quotes from Steven Mitchell's translation of *"An die Musik*/To Music" by Rainer Maria Rilke in *Ahead of All Parting* (New York: Modern Library, 1995).

"music in time," after William L. Benzon, *Beethoven's Anvil* (New York: Basic Books, 2001).

The lyrics of "this song" and "I am" are crafted after the Scottish and English ballads collected and anthologized by Francis James Child in the latter half of the 1800s.

Versions of "Apple Cake" from Russia's Pale of Settlement became a staple in Toronto's Palmerston Avenue Jewish-immigrant community in the early decades of the twentiethth century. But Mother was right—peel those apples for better cake texture.

"Translation and Interpretation 101" erases from page 101 of Umberto Eco, *Experiences in Translation*, translated by Alistair McEwen (Toronto: University of Toronto Press, 2001).

"stories" after William S. Burroughs, "Thanksgiving Prayer," *Tornado Alley* (Cherry Valley, NY: Cherry Valley Editions, 1989).

"with resolve to resolve" alludes to the Jewish holy days that occur towards autumn in the Northern hemisphere. The ten days of reflection between *Rosh Hashana* [Hebrew: New Year, literally head of the year] and *Yom Kippur* [Hebrew: Day of Atonement] are called *Yamim Nora'im* [Hebrew: Days of Awe].

"s[p]in cycle" references repentance and atonement in the *Tashlich* [Hebrew: cast off] Jewish New Year ritual of throwing crusts of bread, symbolically imbued with sins, into a body of water.

"invigilation" after "The Story of the Day" in *Faithful and Virtuous Night* by Louise Glück (Manchester: Carcanet, 2014).

"diethylstilbestrol (DES)" after *Completed Field Notes: The Long Poems of Robert Kroetch* (1927–2011) (Toronto: Longman, 1989).

"questions before and after understanding" after C. G. Jung, *Memories, Dreams and Reflections*, (A. Jaffé, Recorded and Edited (New York: Pantheon, 1973) and J. Kabat-Zinn, *Wherever You Go, There You Are* (New York: Hyperion, 2005).

"silence" quotes from the *Guardian* interview with Ai Weiwei: "Life is never guaranteed to be safe," http://www.youtube.com/watch?v=85t6o_2wFuI, 3:20, published 6 April 2011, http://www.guardian.co.uk.

"How to have a good death in Canada circa 2020" salutes D. Gordon's (1999) "Ten Tips for Better Health" in Dennis Raphael, *Social Determinants of Health: Canadian Perspectives* (Toronto: Canadian Scholars' Press Inc., 2004).

"negotiating death" quotes and misquotes from Margaret Atwood's lecture collection, *Negotiating with the Dead: A Writer on Writing* (Cambridge: Cambridge University Press, 2002).

Created in memoriam for Priscila Uppal, "writing prompt" now also commemorates victims of the COVID-19 pandemic, those left bereft in its wake, and all essential workers who served day after day after day.

"poem paths" responds to "how poets view poetry," a prompt from dee Hobsbawn Smith in the League of Canadian Poets St@nz@ newsletter for National Poetry Month 2015 when she served as Writer in Residence at the Saskatoon Public Library.

Gratitude

Land is sacred. The island where I was born and the land where I now live and write have sustained human activity for thousands of years. I'm grateful for the opportunity to live, work, and contribute where I do. I'm also mindful of unfulfilled covenants with Indigenous peoples everywhere regarding broken lives, lands, and cultures that must be repaired and restored.

Thank you to Luciana Ricciutelli and Inanna Publications for hatching these poems that were brewed with the Algonquin Square Table, Kenneth Sherman and his coterie, Michael Fraser and the Plasticine Poets, Allan Briesmaster and the Vaughn Poets, Stuart Ross and Lillian Allen, then polished in formal mentorships granted by Arc Poetry (Marilyn Dumont) and the Sage Hill Writing Experience (Steven Heighton) in the context of moral support from Molly Peacock, Robyn Sarah, Olive Senior, Merlin Homer, and the PULP Literature editorial crew. Thank you to David Clink, Anne Bindernagel, and Darrell Reimer for reading early manuscript drafts, Adam Sol for generously reading multiple drafts, and Sheila Stewart for proofing final versions. Thank you to friends and relatives who support my writing habit and writers who live in or visit Toronto.

I thank editors and publishers who chose earlier versions of these poems:
Ars Medica: "homage to music therapy" and "Bubba"
Carousel: "summer doesn't notice"
Edition: "it all starts at the kitchen table"
Ensemble: "Failing suicide"
Existere: "stories"
Feathertale Review: "some conditions apply"

Grain: "writing prompt"
Jones Ave: "falling"
Literary Review of Canada: "Tosca" and "Apple Cake"
Misunderstandings Magazine: "masquerade"
Pulp Literature: "the Siren's tale" and *"Taraxacum officinale"*
Saskatoon Public Library: "poem paths"
The Caribbean Writer: *"puertorriqueña,"* "take me home," and "Christiansted, USVI, May 2019"
The Windsor Review: "Translation and Interpretation 101" and "invigilation"
Another Dysfunctional Cancer Poem Anthology (Mansfield Press) "diethylstilbestrol (DES)"
The Art of Poetic Inquiry anthology (Backalong Books): "questions before and after understanding," "n = 24," and "a postphilosophy rant"
Close to Quitting Time anthology (Ascent Aspirations) "Case Closed"
Everything I Couldn't Tell You anthology (Spiderbones Performing Arts): "sonata," "music while dying," "Failing suicide," "music forces its way out," and "music remembers"

I dedicate this collection to the loving memory of Leonard Feigman with gratitude for his steadfast support of me and my creative pursuits.

Photo: Dahlia Katz

Puerto Rican-Canadian María Helena Auerbach Rykov lives in Toronto. Her writing appears online and on paper in numerous venues. More at mary.rykov.com.